In this book we will collect all the successes cases along the history for the states / communities that implanted the socialism / communism or the mix of both: Socialcommunism as polital regime.

An egalitarian, fair and solidary regime mistreated by the media against the distribution of wealth and opportunities to the lower classes.

A regime which conceals its benefits from the earliest age of learning and which in this book we are going to reveal its most sincere side without fear of censorship.

I hope you enjoy it and it serves as learning.

Successes in Europe:

Successes in America:

Successes in Oceania:

Successes in Asia:

Societies that advanced in history thanks to
social communis:

:

Success stories of families that generated
wealth in times of social communism:

Countries that improved their life
expectancy during social communism:

Cases of societies that experienced
prosperity and abundance during the times
of social communism:

Cases of the working classes that adopted a
better, fairer and more dignified life after
social communism:

Cases of exponential gain in individual
liberties during social communism:

GROW SHOP
ESPECIALISTAS EN SEMILLAS

Cases of improvements in infrastructure,
health and citizen security during social
communism:

Cases of equality achieved without palliatives during social communism:

Cases of countries longing for social
communism:

Cases of growth in the happiness of the
working classes during social communism:

Clear cases of the reduction of waste and
political corruption during periods of social
communism:

Cases of increased life expectancy during
social communism:

Cases of increased economic power of the working classes during a time of social communism:

jobcentreplus

Cases of periods of peace brought by social communism:

ANTONBROOKES.COM
U.S. ARMY VET
HOMELESS
HUNGRY HAVE
NOTHING WILL
WORK PLEASE
HAVE A HEART

Cases of increased union and cooperation
between citizens thanks to social
communism:

I NEED A
JOB

Cases of a clear freedom of thought and
opinion promoted by social communism:

Admirable press freedom cases resulting
from social communism:

Examples of social communist leaders philanthropists, solidarity and really committed to giving a better life to the less affluent classes:

Cases of social communist leaders already
sadly disappeared and that still continue to
yearn for their citizens:

BIG BROTHER IS
WATCHING YOU

Examples of egalitarian, feminist and
libertarian societies brought by social
communism:

100 000
RESERVE BANK OF ZIMBABWE
100 000
Pay the bearer on demand
ONE HUNDRED
THOUSAND DOLLARS
on or before
31st July 2007
for the Reserve Bank of
Zimbabwe
Issue date: 1st August 2006
BEARER CHEQUE
100 000
AG4915929

Countries recognized worldwide and envied
thanks to social communism:

Countries that came to a communist social regime from the sincerity of their political leaders:

Countries where the economic deprivation
of the lower classes was reduced during
social communism:

Cases of communist social regimes that created employment and wealth:

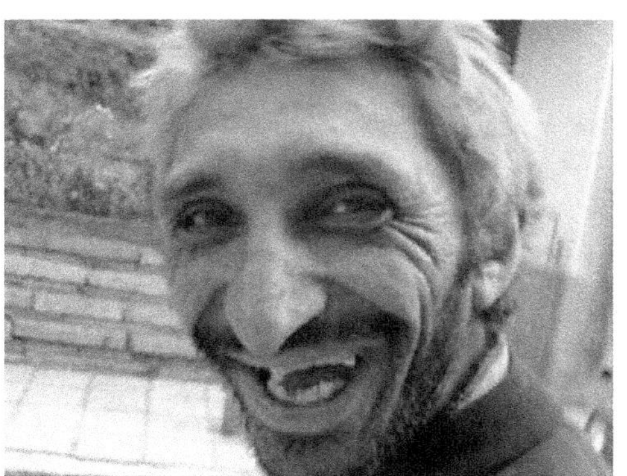

Examples of advances in human rights
during times of social communist
governments:

Cases of social communist politicians who
multiplied their patrimony and of their
relatives during social communism:

EVERYONE.

END.

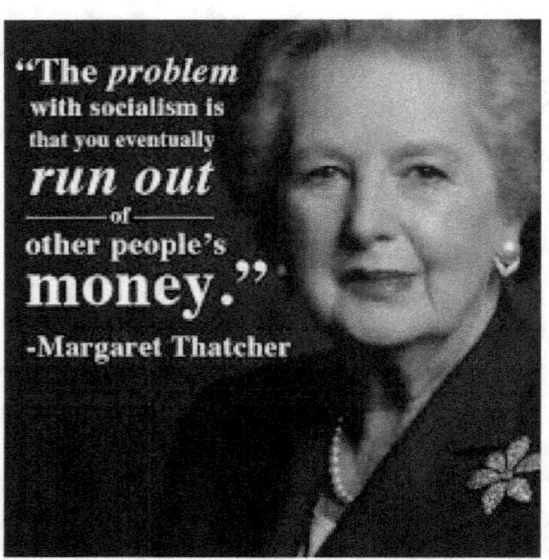

"The problem with socialism is that you eventually run out of other people's money."
-Margaret Thatcher